All Scripture references taken from the KJV of the Holy Bible, unless otherwise indicated.

Every Evil Bird,

by Dr. Marlene Miles

Freshwater Press, 2023

ISBN: 978-1-960150-74-5

Copyright 2023 by Dr. Marlene Miles

All rights reserved. No part of this book may be reproduced, distributed or transmitted by any means or in any means including photocopying, recording or other electronic or mechanical methods without prior written permission of the publisher except in the case of brief publications or critical reviews.

Table of Contents

- Repent 5
- **Holy Ghost Fire** 6
- **Enemies of Destiny** 8
- **Take Dominion** 24
- **Types of Witchcraft Birds** 28
- **Weapons Against Evil Birds** 32
- **Evil Birds: Shut Your Mouths** 44
- **I Condemn You** 47
- **Psalm 7** 51
- **Monitoring Birds** 55
- **Dear Reader:** 72
- **Acknowledgements** 73
- **Other books by this author** 74

Every Evil Bird

This day will the LORD deliver thee into mine hand; and I will smite thee, and take thine head from thee; and I will give the carcasses of the host of the Philistines this day unto the fowls of the air, and to the wild beasts of the earth; that all the earth may know that there is a God in Israel.

(1 Samuel 17:46)

Repent

Lord, I come before You today in prayer. In the Name of Jesus, I ask You to accept my repentance for all my sins. Sins of omission, sins of commission, sins of my youth, frivolity and foolishness, and rebellion. Sins that I've committed knowingly and unknowingly, in the Name of Jesus.

Lord, I repent also for my parents and my ancestors, all the way back to Adam and Eve--, even before Adam and Eve, where I retrieve my essence, in the Name of Jesus.

Holy Ghost Fire

Holy Ghost Fire fall on me now, in the Name of Jesus. (X3)

Holy Ghost Power to disgrace every bird of darkness, come upon me now, in the Name of Jesus.

I receive power to scatter the agenda of evil birds against my destiny, this year, in the Name of Jesus.

Any evil power troubling my destiny, scatter, in the Name of Jesus.

O God arise and set my life in order today. Do something that will make my enemy cry, in the Name of Jesus.

Lord, change my life for good, by Fire, by Fire, by Fire, in the Name of Jesus.

Evil powers placing my destiny on chill, on lockdown, or in a cooler, lose your power and scatter, in the Name of Jesus.

Enemies of Destiny

Every enemy of my destiny, the Lord Jesus correct you and deal ruthlessly with you, in the Name of Jesus.

My destiny, come alive by Fire. My destiny, come alive by Fire. My destiny, come alive by Fire. My God-given destiny, come alive, by Fire. My original destiny, come alive by Fire, by Fire, by Fire, in the Name of Jesus. (X7)

Any evil bird that has come for the Word of God so that it not take root in my heart, scatter, in the Name of Jesus.

Birds of distraction, you will not succeed; my face is set like flint, my focus is on the Lord, you will not succeeed, you will not distract me, in the Name of Jesus.

Any evil bird that has come for the Word of God that it not grow in my heart, I reject you--, I reject you, I reject you. You will not take the Word from my heart, in the Name of Jesus. The Word of God is forever established in my heart, in Jesus' Name.

Birds of destruction, I destroy you by the Thunder Fire, Thunder Fire, Thunder Fire – the Thunder Fire of God, in the Name of Jesus.

Greedy birds, ravenous birds, unclean birds, you are an abomination to God, the Lord rebuke you. Scatter, scatter, scatter from my life, in the Name of Jesus.

Every evil bird employed by powers of darkness you shall not tamper with the Word of God in my heart. You shall not tamper with me, my family, my life and my destiny, in the Name of Jesus. ***Return to sender***, in Jesus' Mighty Name.

Any power blocking me from starting a new project, I crush your blockades and blockages now with the Thunder Hammer of God, in the Name of Jesus.

Any destructive force or power trying to undo projects I have already begun, trying to block my progress, I deprogram you, I dismantle your assignment and I rebuke your agency to work against me, by the power in the Blood of Jesus.

Every evil bird after my seed... (any type of seed), the Word of God, good ideas, my family, my children, all financial seeds --, I command you to scatter. Be gone, and die, in the Name of Jesus.

I bind and paralyze the *spirit of anger* which invites angry birds into my life, and prevents me from getting rid of them, in the Name of Jesus.

Every evil bird masquerading as a beautiful bird, as a pretty bird, as a curious or interesting bird, **DIE** in the Name of Jesus.

Lord, give me immunity from witchcraft dragnets, by the Blood, by the Power in the Blood of Jesus, in the Name of Jesus.

Every evil bird perched in my environment to have a look at me, or monitor me, go blind and fall from your perch, in the Name of Jesus.

Every satanic bird, I strip you of your powers by Fire, by Fire, in the Name of Jesus.

Every wicked bird sent to pollute my environment, to pollute me or my life, crash and burn, in the Name of Jesus.

Every evil bird sent to transmit words, messages, spells, curses or just to torment or intimidate me, return to sender, and then die, in the Name of Jesus.

Wicked birds sent to damage me, my property, my life or destiny--, either physically or spiritually, be hit by a lightning bolt of God and combust, in the Name of Jesus.

Every satanic, robotic, programmed, evil flying bird flying in my direction fall down and die, in the Name of Jesus.

Every satanic bird flying in my direction, I burn your travel route with the Fire of the Holy Ghost; fall down and die, fall down and die, fall down and die, in the Name of Jesus.

Every evil bird programmed by witchcraft personalities; Lord let that personality be trapped forever in that bird, in the Name of Jesus.

Lord, give me ears to hear and eyes to see every evil bird, whether visble or invisible, in the Name of Jesus.

Wicked birds sent to steal, kill and destroy--, die in the Name of Jesus.

Every evil bird sent to bewitch--, bewitch yourself, in the Name of Jesus.

Every evil bird sent to afflict me, **find your sender** and afflict them 7X more.

Lord, correct their evil by their own wickedness, in the Name of Jesus.

Every bird sent to feed me with food or beverage, drink your own blood, eat your own flesh and perish, in the Name of Jesus.

Any oppressive heaviness as the result of evil bird attack, Mighty Hand of God, oppress the birds, and deal with them ruthlessly.

I shake off every oppression, in the Name of Jesus. (X3)

Every sudden pain attack, **back to sender, 7-fold** so they know that JESUS IS LORD. (X3 or more)

Every attack of fear and anxiety, back to sender, in the Name of Jesus.

Every threat trying to take away my breath–, God breathed this life in me; He breathed this breath in me. This is *my* breath that God gave me, you'll take nothing, nothing from me, by the power in the Blood of Jesus. I command, **FAILED MISSION, FAILED MISSION** against me. Back to sender, you go back to your sender, and you give *them* what was intended for me, in Jesus' Name.

Every evil bird after the brain, mind, or cognitive functions, you shall not capture my mind or head, in the Name of Jesus.

Every attack of blank mind, forgetfulness, or forgotten words, back to sender, in the Name of Jesus.

Bird of Satan delegated against my breakthrough, hands off my blessings, hands off my successes and hands off my breakthroughs--, and then die, in the Name of Jesus.

Birds of sleep wave designed to lull me to sleep at the wrong time, you need to die, in the Name of Jesus.

Every foul odor related to evil birds, I reject you; I rebuke you. Wind of God blow the foul odor and the birds away, never to return to my life again, in the Name of Jesus.

Sweet fragrance and perfume and favor of God, fall on me, surround me and my life, in the Name of Jesus.

Evil birds of memory loss, forget my name and lose my address, in the spirit and in the natural, in the Name of Jesus.

Evil birds of brain fog and mental confusion, back to sender, back to sender, back to sender, back to sender, back to sender, back to sender, 7-fold, in Jesus' Name.

Evil birds of dizziness, back to sender. Just go crazy, fly in circles, then fall down and die, in the Name of Jesus.

Urinating, defecating, foul, unclean, evil birds sent to pollute my property, business, house, life, degrees, diplomas, certificates--, roast to ashes, in the Name of Jesus.

You evil birds of Satan, I arrest you in the Spirit and render your mission canceled, in the Name of Jesus. Fall down and die. (X5)

> Behold, all they that were incensed against thee shall be ashamed and confounded: they shall be as nothing; and they that strive with thee shall perish.
>
> Thou shalt seek them, and shalt not find them, even them that contended with thee: they that war against thee shall be as nothing, and as a thing of nought. (Isaiah 41:11-12)

Lord, I use every violent weapon of warfare against every evil bird sent in my direction, in the Name of Jesus.

Lord, open Your armory and bring out weapons of Your righteous indignation against every evil bird that is sent against me, in the Name of Jesus.

Blood of Jesus.

Name of Jesus.

Word of God.

Fire of the Holy Spirit.

The Word of my testimony; I am an overcomer in Christ. I am more than a conqueror in Christ Jesus.

I release a **thick fog** into the camps of the enemy and a **cloud of confusion** on every evil bird--, be confused, be perpetually confused, in the Name of Jesus.

Thunder of God

Thunder Lightning of God

Lightning of God, strike them, strike them, strike them. Strike them down, strike them dead, in the Name of Jesus.

I decree blindness upon every evil bird sent against me, in the Name of Jesus.

I send **double destruction** to every wicked, witchcraft bird in my environment, in the Name of Jesus.

I declare darkness over you. God created light; Father, take away their light and their visibility, in the Name of Jesus.

I break you off, every evil bird; I break you off from your network, lose your signal; lose your power, in the Name of Jesus.

Arrow of God, pierce them through with many arrows, every evil bird that has come to steal kill or destroy from me, Arrow of God pierce them through with many arrows, in Jesus' Name.

Dark birds of wickedness, I drive you into uninhabitable wilderness, in the Name of Jesus.(X2)

Mighty Warrior Angels of GOD fight for me, fight with me, in the Name of Jesus as I fight against these evil birds.

Every satanic bird flying against my breakthroughs, fall down and die, in the Name of Jesus.

> So shall they fear the name of the LORD from the west, and his glory from the rising of the sun. When the enemy shall come in like a flood, the Spirit of the LORD shall lift up a standard against him. (Isaiah 59:19)

Every satanic bird of my father's house, die, in the Name of Jesus.

Every satanic bird of my mother's house, die, in the Name of Jesus.

Every satanic bird of my ex's house--, my in-laws' house, my ex-in laws' house, any relative, any friend or fake friend, and *whosoever*. Any satanic bird of any whosoever's house, anyone who would even send an evil bird in my direction, let the arrows of the Lord's wrath find them, in the Name of Jesus.

Every bird of darkness assigned against my house, die, die, die, in the Name of Jesus.

Every satanic bird assigned against my finances, health, education, marriage, family, children, profession, ministry, purpose and destiny, die, die, die, in the Name of Jesus.

Birds of darkness, carry your evil loads, in the Name of Jesus.

Every witchcraft bird assigned against my fruitfulness, pregnancy, gestation, birth, or placenta, die, in the Name of Jesus.

Every evil bird assigned after my child or children, die mercilessly, in the Name of Jesus.

Every evil bird after my husband, or wife, collapse on your way to my spouse and die, in the Name of Jesus.

You, satanic birds, release your arrow on your senders and not me, in the Name of Jesus.

Every evil bird sent to tamper with or steal my worship to God, scatter, in the Name of Jesus. I will worship the Lord. Amen.

Every evil bird that has swallowed my blessings, successes, or virtues, vomit them up now and then die, in the Name of jesus.

Evil birds swallowing the good things in my life, choke, retch and vomit it all out, and then die, in the Name of Jesus. (X2)

He that has swallowed down riches,
he shall vomit them up again.

(Job 20:15)

God, cast all my goodness out of the belly of every evil bird, in the Name of Jesus. (X3)

Evil birds swallowing my fortunes and good successes, become bloated and explode. Lord, cleanse all my good blessings and fortunes with Living Water and return them to me, please, in the Name of Jesus. Amen.

Take Dominion

Lord, I take Dominion over all the works of your hands, birds of the air, -- everything You created.

Until I know which birds are real, which are fake and which ones are evil, let me walk in the Dominion and authority that you created and set me in, in the Name of Jesus.

Lord, if I have swallowed any bird, knowingly or unknowingly, I vomit it out now, I vomit it out, I vomit it out, I vomit it out, I vomit it out, in the Name of Jesus. Light has no communion with darkness, in Jesus' Name.

Every satanic bird that is barking, chirping, pecking, flapping, cawing, squawking, secreting excrement of any kind against my prosperity, die, in the Name of Jesus.

Every egg of witchcraft laid on my life, break and come to nothing, in the Name of Jesus.

Every evil bird flying against my destiny, fall down and die, in the Name of Jesus.

Every vulture of death assigned against me, die, in the Name of Jesus.

Every vulture of death assigned against me, I command: **FAILED ASSIGNMENT;** vulture, *you* die, in the Name of Jesus.

Every bird of assassination, you die in the Name of Jesus.

You, satanic birds, vomit my prosperity, in the Name of Jesus.

Every evil bird, fall down and die (X7)

Every evil bird sent flying against me in the day or night, either visible or invisible, I command you to fly into electric lines and be electrocuted, in the Name of Jesus. Be they visible or spiritual electirc lines, fly into them, be electrocuted, and die, in the Name of Jesus.

Every evil bird at any window of my house or business, fall down and die, in the Name of Jesus.

Every evil bird making any evil, satanic, unknown or not understood noises in the day or night, lose your voice, lose your voice, lose your voice, and croak, in the Name of Jesus.

Every evil bird on the roof of my house or the roof of my business, or shop, I belong to Jesus Christ, I am none of your business – fly or die, fly or die, fly away or die, fly or die, fly or die, in the Name of Jesus.

Types of Witchcraft Birds

Baby Witchcraft Birds, the Lord restrain you from acting out evil against me, in the Name of Jesus.

Any strange objects in my body, programmed by any kind of witchcraft, come out, come out, come out, be expelled, be disintegrated, become useless and non-functional and do not hurt me in any way in the process, in the Name of Jesus.

Every wicked witchcraft in my family be disgraced--, cease and desist, in the Name of Jesus.

Household witchcraft, stand down, stand down, stand down, or incur the wrath of God, in the Name of Jesus.

Moderate evil birds sent to torment or afflict me, lose your powers, lose your direction, lose your assignment, in the Name of Jesus.

Any and every evil bird sent to cage me, my property or my destiny--, fall down and die. Fall down and die, defeated, in the Name of Jesus.

I bind & paralyze every *desert spirit* against me, no matter its origin, in the Name of Jesus. (X3)

Blood sucking evil birds, I arrest you in the Spirit and I crush you, without Mercy, with the Thunder Hammer of God, in the Name of Jesus. (X2)

Munchhausen by proxy birds – birds doing the damage but pretending to help – you are a **LIAR**, fall down with your lies, and die, in the Name of Jesus.

Satanic birds, I am not your horse, you are not my rider—get off me! GET OFF ME! GET OFF me, in the Mighty Name of Jesus Christ.

Warrior Angels of God, do your worst against those who are evil, unrelenting, or are too powerful for me, in the Name of Jesus. (X3)

Evil birds, I am not your candidate, I am not your sacrifice, I am not your food or beverage--, die, in the Name of Jesus.

I bind every type of witchcraft from operating against me, my life, my house, my family, ministry, career and destiny, and I paralyze them, in the Name of Jesus.

Lord, build a wall of fire, a hedge of fire, a mountain of fire around me, my family and everything under my stewardship so that it is **too hot, too hot, too hot** for every evil bird of any type, denomination, origin, or occultic level, in the Name of Jesus.

Mother Birds, Father Birds, the Blood of Jesus precludes you from operating against me, in the Name of Jesus.

Weapons Against Evil Birds

Every evil bird must die. every evil bird must die. Every evil bird must die. evil bird must die, Evil birds must die, evil birds must die, in the Name of Jesus.

I throw divine stones of Fire at you, and I do not miss my target, in the Name of Jesus. (x3)

I throw:

Divine Stones of Fire

Holy Ghost Molotov cocktails

Hailstones of Fire

FIRE! FIRE! FIRE!!!!

Every evil bird, receive Fire, receive the Fire of God, receive the Fire that is in the Blood of Jesus.

Lord, make me and all that is mine too hot, too hot to handle, in the Name of Jesus.

My life, receive Fire; become Fire in the Name of Jesus. (X3)

I roast all wicked satanic birds; I roast them I roast them. I roast them. I roast them I roast them, in the Name of Jesus.

Every bird of darkness working against me, fall down and die, in Jesus' Name.

I arrest every evil bird against my breakthroughs, in the Name of Jesus.

I fire back every arrow of evil birds, I fire them back, in the Name of Jesus.

every arrow, every arrow, every arrow!!! I fire them back, in the Name of Jesus.

Familiar spirits, peepers and mutterers, I bind and paralyze you from working against me; I arrest your powers, in the Name of Jesus.

Every habitation of witchcraft birds--, especially against my life, become desolate, in the Name of Jesus.

Every bird of darkness on assignment against my destiny be roasted by Holy Ghost Fire, in the Name of Jesus.

My life, jump out of every inherited witchcraft cage, in the Name of Jesus. (X2)

I am not your candidate-, you eaters of flesh and drinkers of blood, I am not your candidate; eat your own flesh, drink your own blood, in Jesus Name. My family, my children, my spouse, we are not your candidates, eat your own flesh, drink your own blood, and die, in the Name of Jesus.

Holy Ghost Fire, barricade my habitation from the rage of satanic birds, in the Name of Jesus.

My destiny, reject every bewitchment sent against me by the birds of darkness, in the Name of Jesus.

My life, become untouchable to every bird of darkness, in the Name of Jesus.

My life, receive Fire, become Fire in the Name of Jesus. (X7)

Any power or any evil against me using any evil bird, be dismantled, in Jesus' Name.

My virtues, swallowed by satanic birds, be vomited, in the Name of Jesus.

Power of the night coming against me; be disgraced, in the Name of Jesus.

Every monitoring bird of darkness, formed and sent against me, be disgraced and your charms be deprogrammed, and your assignment be dismantled, in the Name of Jesus.

I shall destroy every company of Satanic birds directed against me, by the Power in the Blood of Jesus, in the Name of Jesus.

Every witchcraft bird flying against my destiny, fly no more, in Jesus' Name.

Holy Ghost Fire. Burn away the memory of my life from every evil bird, in the Name of Jesus.

Every evil cry against me or near my house, at night, be silenced; SHUT UP, in the Name of Jesus.

God arise, and let all my stubborn enemies scatter, in the Name of Jesus.

Every evil bird sent to monitor me, or has been programmed for affliction against me, or into my life, fall down and die, mercilessly, in the Name of Jesus.

Prayers against every evil bird, Lord thank You for hearing them and answering them, in the Name of Jesus.

Every shouting, evil bird sent in my direction, East Wind of God, blow them down from the sky, or from their perch, and let them die, in the Name of Jesus.

Every evil bird that is a *witchcraft spirit*, I disconnect you from your network; fall down and die, in the Name of Jesus.

Every evil bird containing an evil serpent, be struck with the Thunder-

Lightning of God. Be executed, without mercy, and die immediately, in the Name of Jesus.

Every Evil bird shouting aloud to arrest or divert my blessings, shut your mouth, in the Name of Jesus.

Any monitoring or attack from an owl, a vulture, or a bat, I arrest you, in the Spirit with prayers and fasting, in the Name of Jesus.

Powers sending witchcraft birds in my environment, fail against me, fail against me, fail against me, in the Name of Jesus. Return to sender.

Let all attacks happen to your senders--, not to me, in the Name of Jesus.

Shouting, witchcraft birds--, shut your evil mouths. I will not listen to the words of the devil today or the words of the enemy today. They will have no effect on me. Evil words will have no effect on me, today, by the Power in the Blood of Jesus.

Evil birds, every evil bird, **choke on your words, choke on your words, choke on your noises, your sounds, your squawks, your chirps, your peeps, your mutters, and** return to sender, in the Name of Jesus.

Night birds, get away from my windows. Get away from my doors, in the Name of Jesus.

You cannot have my glory. You cannot have my glory, you cannot have my glory. You cannot have my birthright. You cannot have my inheritance, in Christ. You cannot have my blessings, or successes. Take your evil assignment back to your senders and capture *them*, in the Name of Jesus.

   Witchcraft agents,

   Monitoring *spirits*,

Satanic agents,

Marine agents,

Household agents

Environmental agents,

Village agents, Town agents, Community agents, Local evil agents

Graveyard agents,

Evil altar agents,

All agents of destruction, I bind and paralyze your ability to work against me, by the Resurrection power of Jesus Christ, and by the Blood of the Lamb, in the Name of Jesus. Amen.

Powers of darkness sent to release the *spirit of anxiety*, I reject it, I reject it, I reject it, I reject it, in the Name of Jesus. Go back and release it on your senders. Make them anxious, nervous and very afraid for the **King of Glory** who is strong and mighty in battle will contend with them. Have them to be very afraid, in the Name of Jesus.

I dwell in safety, and I sleep because the Lord gives me sleep. I reject your attempts of depriving me of sleep, in the Name of Jesus.

Destiny-stealing, destiny-diverting evil birds, progress-hindering evil birds, wasters of divine opportunities--, the Lord Jesus rebuke you. Return to sender, in the Name of Jesus.

Birds representing the Prince of Persia, as in the Book of Daniel, I call for divine help from the Archangel Michael to withstand you, against me, and my answers to prayer, and my breakthroughs, in the Name of Jesus.

Birds converting the night into spiritual warfare, Angels of God, Jehovah Sabaoth, fight my battles for me, in the Name of Jesus.

Birds trying to make me run in circles and waste time, you go *loco* and fall down and die, in the Name of Jesus.

Birds sent to bite me at the point of breakthrough; return to sender, 7-fold. Go back and bite your senders, in the Name of Jesus.

Birds sent to cause spontaneous abortion, my God declares that there shall be no barren among His people; and I am **His people**-, abort your mission; abort yourself, you abort nothing about me or my life, in the Name of Jesus.

Birds sent to take away the memory of my helper, I resist your attacks with the shield of Faith and declare that the memory of my destiny helpers will not be cut off, in the Name of Jesus.

Birds sent to blind spiritual eyes—it is the Lord who gives me vision and sight, it is not up for grabs, go back, go back, go back to your owners for it is their sin that will make them spiritually blind, in the Name of Jesus.

Birds that are messengers of sorrow; there is no work for you here, you are fired; go and mourn the loss of your sender, in the Name of Jesus.

Birds sent to eat up the sacrifices intended for the Lord--, the Lord takes good pleasure in my offerings, first fruits and sacrifices. Let the power of my sacrifice and the power in the greatest sacrifice of all time, Jesus Christ, speak for me; let The Blood speak for me, in the Name of Jesus. Amen.

Evil, murdering *spirits*, the Lord rebuke you, you will not prosper here tonight, this night, any day or night; return to sender, in the Name of Jesus.

Evil Birds: Shut Your Mouths

Birds that say I can go nowhere, shut your mouth, in the Name of Jesus.

Birds that utter curses, shut your mouth, in the Name of Jesus.

Birds that say I can rise no more than this--, shut your mouth, in the Name of Jesus.

Birds that say you have been captured; shut your mouth, in the Name of Jesus.

Birds that say your expectations, or my expectations have been cut short; shut your mouth, in the Name of Jesus.

Birds that come against your marriage, birds that come against your marriage or my marriage, shut your mouth, in the Name of Jesus.

I command the night so that birds that come to eat up my blessings of the next day will not be successful.

Shut your mouth; you shall not eat up my blessings, in the Name of Jesus.

Birds of untimely death, shut your mouth, and you die instead, in the Name of Jesus.

Birds of sickness and affliction, shut your mouth, in the Name of Jesus.

Birds of failure; shut your mouth, in the Name of Jesus.

Birds announcing satanic torment, I bind the *spirits of torment and affliction* and by the Blood of Jesus I preclude it from working against me and my family, in the Name of Jesus.

I Condemn You

Behold, they shall surely gather together, but not by me: whosoever shall gather together against thee shall fall for thy sake.

Behold, I have created the smith that bloweth the coals in the fire, and that bringeth forth an instrument for his work; and I have created the waster to destroy.

No weapon that is formed against thee shall prosper; and every tongue that shall rise against thee in judgment thou shalt condemn. This is the heritage of the servants of the LORD, and their righteousness is of me, saith the LORD. (Isaiah 54:15-17)

Gathering birds, I condemn you, in the Name of Jesus. **Scatter**, in the Name of Jesus.

Gathering birds, gathering to make my life, ministry or business suffer, I condemn you, in the Name of Jesus. **Scatter,** in the Name of Jesus.

Flapping birds, birds trying to get into my house, I condemn you, in the Name of Jesus.

Go to the Abyss from where you cannot return, you and the powers that sent you. Go! I declare: **FAILED ASSIGNMENT;** go to the Abyss, in the Name of Jesus.

I surrender all to you, Jesus Christ. I repent of every known sin, in the Name of Jesus.

I renounce sin and every evil covenant formed as a result of sin, in the Name of Jesus.

Evil birds crying against my elevation, roast by Fire, in the Name of Jesus.

Satanic birds coveting or covering my glory, today I set you ablaze, in the Name of Jesus.

Evil birds picking up the Word of God from my Spirit, fall down and die, in the Name of Jesus.

Every witchcraft bird singing a song of affliction against my glory, or against my person, shut up and roast by Fire, in the Name of Jesus.

I destroy every evil bird organizing a witchcraft meeting on the roof of my house, on the roof of my business, or anywhere near my house or business, in the Name of Jesus.

Any satanic birds swallowing my virtues, be vomited now by Fire, in the Name of Jesus.

Psalm 7

A psalm of David, which he sang to the LORD concerning Cush of the tribe of Benjamin.

I come to you for protection,
O LORD my God.
Save me from my persecutors—
rescue me!

If you don't, they will maul me like a lion,
tearing me to pieces with no one to

rescue me.

O LORD my God, if I have done
wrong
or am guilty of injustice,
if I have betrayed a friend
or plundered my enemy without
cause,
then let my enemies capture me.

Let them trample me into the ground
and drag my honor in the dust.
Arise, O LORD, in anger!

Stand up against the fury of my
enemies!
Wake up, my God, and bring
justice!

Gather the nations before you.
Rule over them from on high.

The LORD judges the nations.
Declare me righteous, O LORD,
  for I am innocent, O Most High!

End the evil of those who are wicked,
  and defend the righteous.
For you look deep within the mind
  and heart,
  O righteous God.

God is my shield,
  saving those whose hearts are true
  and right.

God is an honest judge.
He is angry with the wicked every
  day.

If a person does not repent,
  God will sharpen his sword;
he will bend and string his bow.

He will prepare his deadly weapons
and shoot his flaming arrows.

The wicked conceive evil;
they are pregnant with trouble
and give birth to lies.

They dig a deep pit to trap others,
then fall into it themselves.

The trouble they make for others
backfires on them.
The violence they plan falls on
their own heads.

I will thank the Lord because he is
just;
I will sing praise to the name of
the Lord Most High.

AMEN.

Monitoring Birds

Every monitoring bird against my progress, receive total blindness and die, in the Name of Jesus.

Every household bird programmed to make life difficult for me, receive the flaming arrow of **death**, in the Name of Jesus.

O God arise and trouble those using evil birds to trouble my destiny, in the Name of Jesus.

Every bird that is flying against my fruitfulness, die, in the Name of Jesus. Household enemies using satanic birds to fight me, I destroy those birds by Fire and by Thunder, in the Name of Jesus.

Every attack of witchcraft birds against me, catch Fire, in the Name of Jesus.

Every evil bird attaching themselves to my glory, I break the ties--, I break them by Fire, in the Name of Jesus.

Any power in my neighborhood manifesting themselves as evil birds at night to pursue me, scatter by Fire, scatter by Fire, scatter by Fire, in the Name of Jesus.

My life has become Fire and I receive Fire, in the Name of Jesus.

Arrows of strange birds fired into my life, backfire, in the Name of Jesus.

Evil birds whispering or squawking my name to the witchcraft coven, burn to ashes, in the Name of Jesus. Burn before you can speak, in the Name of Jesus.

Every covenant of stagnation programmed against me by the household birds, break by Fire, in the Name of Jesus.

Every evil bird landing at my shop or house, go back to sender, in the Name of Jesus.

O God, let the legs of every satanic bird become hot legs, and have them catch fire, in the Name of Jesus.

I destroy the wings of every evil bird, in the Name of Jesus. I command the sun work on my behalf, let all the elements work in my favor. Sun, melt their wings, in the Name of Jesus.

Fire of God, let all the wings become hot wings, and catch fire, in the Name of Jesus.

Let the legs of every satanic bird catch fire, in the Name of Jesus.

Whatever any evil bird has stolen from me, return it back by Fire, in the Name of Jesus.

You, satanic birds, release my virtues, and die by Fire, in the Name of Jesus.

Every evil bird that flies against me by night, I pull you down, I pull you down, I pull you down, in the Name of Jesus.

Every dark or screeching owl assigned to eat up my flesh, be consumed to ashes, in the Name of Jesus.

All wickedness done to my marriage by any evil birds, backfire today, in the Name of Jesus.

Every evil bird dragging my destiny backward, catch Fire, in the Name of Jesus.

Every evil bird at the garden of my destiny, collide with the Fire of the Holy Ghost and die mysteriously, in the Name of Jesus.

My Father, hide my glory from every satanic bird assigned against my life, in the Name of Jesus.

Any local birds ministering poverty into my soul, spirit or body take your gift and go! Go! And, die, in the Name of Jesus.

Holy Ghost Fire consume the body of all evil birds that are up against my life, in the Name of Jesus.

I set ablaze every evil bird recording my conversations in my house, in the Name of Jesus.

Witchcraft birds from my father's house and mother's house --- *loose* and lose your hold over my life, in the Name of Jesus.

I destroy every habitation of evil birds in my environment, in the Name of Jesus.

O Lord, let every evil bird monitoring my womb, receive the anger of God and release my womb, in the Name of Jesus.

Any power from any environment assigned to bring me down physically or spiritually, die, in the Name of Jesus.

Curses from evil birds, backfire, in the Name of Jesus.

Satanic birds causing delays in my destiny, I destroy you, in the Name of Jesus.

As from today, the voice of evil birds against me, cease by Fire, in the Name of Jesus.

Every evil bird, your opinion, desires, and Words and those of whomever sent you, are not welcome in my life. Go!, in the Name of Jesus.

Every witchcraft mirror, catch Fire, in the Name of Jesus.

Any evil bird sent from the evil forest to swallow my blessings, fall down and die, in Jesus' Name.

I break free and release myself from the attack of every evil bird, in the Name of Jesus.

Any evil bird, every evil bird that has stolen babies from my womb, return them by Fire, in the Name of Jesus.

Any evil bird that has stolen babies from my womb, return them by Fire, in the Name of Jesus. (X5, or more).

Any evil bird that has stolen babies from my womb, return them by Fire and by force, in the Name of Jesus.

My blessings, come out of the body of evil birds, in the Name of Jesus.

Every cyclical, weekly, or monthly visitation of satanic birds against me, I cancel it today, by the Blood of Jesus.

O God, expose any evil personality using demonic birds against my progress, in the Name of Jesus.

Evil birds crying while flapping their wings, receive the Fire arrows of destruction, in the Name of Jesus.

Evil birds against my promotion, be disgraced, in the Name of Jesus.

Ancestral evil bird become deaf and dumb forever concerning my destiny, in the Name of Jesus.

Lord, have my blessings take the path which no fowl knows, even the vulture's eye has not seen it, in the Name of Jesus. (X2)

Thank You, Jesus for saving me from my enemies, in the Name of Jesus.

Evil bird travelling with me to monitor me, die on your way, in Jesus' Name.

Father, let this witchcraft bird roast by Fire, in the Name of Jesus.

Ancestral evil bird, become deaf and dumb forever concerning me, in Jesus' Name.

Every household bird following me from tree to tree, die by Fire, in the Name of Jesus.

Any witchcraft bird assigned to torment me day and night, die by Fire, in Jesus' Name. (X2)

Any problem that I am passing through now that is caused by evil birds, O God arise, contend with them, and sentence them to death by Fire, in the Name of Jesus.

Blood of Jesus separate my destiny from evil birds, in Jesus' Name.

Evil birds whispering my name on a tree, be arrested by Fire; fall down and die, in the Name of Jesus.

Every evil tree monitoring me, turn to ashes and blow away by the East Wind of God, in Jesus' Name.

Lord, blind the eyes of every evil bird that is planning to attack my destiny, in the Name of Jesus.

I bind the operation of evil birds operating against me, in Jesus' Name.

You, evil birds perching on my glory, somersault and scatter by Fire and by Force, in the Name of Jesus.

Evil tree harboring witchcraft birds be struck by the Thunder Fire of the Holy Ghost, in Jesus' Name.

Let the tree you've perched on become too hot for you to perch upon, in the Name of Jesus.

Satanic birds gathered together on a tree against my glory, scatter unto utter desolation, in Jesus' Name.

I paralyze evil birds flying for my sake, (X3) by the power in the Blood of Jesus.

Every evil bird assigned to investigate my future, die by Fire, in Jesus' Name.

Any man, woman, or child using birds to block my ways, let Fire from Heaven visit them and destroy their evil plan. Let Fire destroy their every plan, in Jesus' Name.

Whatever strange birds have eaten that is mine, I command them to be vomited, in Jesus' Name.

All stubborn birds targeting my life and my family's life, die by Fire, in the Name of Jesus Christ.

I renounce and *loose* myself from every negative dedication placed upon my life, in the Name of Jesus.

Evil birds whispering my name in the heavenlies, be arrested by Fire, in Jesus' Name.

Every satanic bird posted to my house to divert my goodness, fall down and die, in the Name of Jesus.

Every evil bird laid upon my life, receive the Fire of God and wither, in the Name of Jesus.

I recover back by Fire and by force everything stolen from me in my days of ignorance, in Jesus' Name. (X2)

Every power assigned to weaken my faith, die now, in Jesus' Name.

Night powers dominating my nights, scatter by Fire, in the Name of Jesus.

Everyone calling my name for evil, fall down and die, in the Name of Jesus. (X3)

Every power ordained to suffocate my destiny, receive Fire and die, in Jesus' Name.

Angels of God search through the land of the living and the dead and recover my lost virtues and goodness; recover it for me, Lord, in Jesus' Name.

Every good thing that is dead in my life, receive life by Fire, in the Name of Jesus.

Let all those having satanic night vigils against me be silenced--, silenced in the grave, in the Name of Jesus.

Anyone that needs to die for me to live long, let them die now, in the Name of Jesus.

I use the Blood of Jesus to cancel any evil that is coming towards me, in Jesus' Name.

Fire of protection cover me and my family and our possessions, in Jesus' Name.

I command all the dark works done against my life in secret to now be exposed and nullified, in the Name of Jesus.

Any part of my body under oppression, receive deliverance by Fire, now, in the Name of Jesus. (X3 or more).

O God arise and embarrass me with miracles and testimonies, in the Name of Jesus.

Lord, I bind up every power, principality, every *spirit* and every source of evil that intends to retaliate against me because of these prayers, in the Name of Jesus.

I seal every declaration and every decree with the Blood of Jesus and with the Holy Ghost, the Spirit of Promise. I seal them across every realm, era, age, timeline and dimension, past, present and future to infinity, in the Name of Jesus.

Thank You, Lord for hearing and answering prayers, in the Name of Jesus.

AMEN.

Dear Reader:

Thank you for choosing and reading this book. It is a prayer book, so I pray that your prayers have reached the ears of God and that your victory is imminent, in the Name of Jesus.

God's Grace to you,

Dr. Marlene Miles

Acknowledgements

Some prayers adapted from or inspired by the book, **Silencing the Birds of Darkness** *by Dr. DK Olukoya, Sister Shade Olukoya did the art for Dr. Olukoya's book.*

Some prayers adapted from or inspired by Minister Joshua Orekhie, who has a number of excellent videos on this subject on Youtube.

Other books by this author

AK: The Adventures of the Agape Kid

AMONG SOME THIEVES

Churchzilla, T*he Wanna-Be, Supposed-to-be Bride of Christ*

Courtroom Prayers @Midnight

Demons Hate Questions

Don't Refuse Me, Lord (4 book series)

Every Evil Bird

Evil Petition in the Court of Accusation

Evil Touch

Evil Petition in the Court of Accusation

The Fold (4 book series)

    The Fold (Book 1)

    Name Your Seed (Book 2)

    The Poor Attitudes of Money (Book 3)

    Do Not Orphan Your Seed

got HEALING? Verses for Life

got LOVE? Verses for Life

got money?

How to Dental Assist

Let Me Have A Dollar's Worth

Man Safari, *The*

Marriage Ed. *Rules of Engagement & Marriage*

Made Perfect in Love

Power Money: Nine Times the Tithe

The Power of Wealth *(forthcoming)*

Seasons of Grief

Seasons of War *(forthcoming)*

The Spirit of Poverty *(forthcoming)*

Triangular Power *(series)*

    Powers Above

    SUNBLOCK

    Do Not Swear by the Moon

    STARSTRUCK

Warfare Prayers Against Beauty Curses

Warfare Prayer Against Poverty

When the Devourer is Rebuked

The Wilderness Romance *(3-book series)*

> *The Social Wilderness*
>
> *The Sexual Wilderness*
>
> *The Spiritual Wilderness*

Journals & Devotionals by this author:

The Cool of the Day – Journal for times with God

He Hears Us, Prayer Journal in 4 colors

I Have A Star, Dream Journal kids, teen, adult

I Have A Star, Guided Prayer Journal, Boy/Girl

J'ai une Etoile, Journal des Reves

Let Her Dream, Dream Journal multiple colors

Men Shall Dream, Dream Journal, (blue or black)

My Favorite Prayers (multiple covers)

My Sowing Journal (in three colors)

Tengo una Estrella, Diario de Sueños

Wise Counsel (Journal in 2 styles)

Illustrated children's books by this author:

Be the Lion (3-book series)

Big Dog (8-book series)

Do Not Say That to Me

Every Apple

Fluff the Clouds

I Love You All Over the World

Imma Dance

The Jump Rope

Kiss the Sun

The Masked Man

Not During a Pandemic

Push the Wind

Slide

Tangled Taffy

What If?

Wiggle, Wiggle; Giggle, Giggle

Worry About Yourself

You Did Not Say Goodbye to Me

www.ingramcontent.com/pod-product-compliance
Lightning Source LLC
Chambersburg PA
CBHW061340040426
42444CB00011B/3018